Read at Home
Handbook

Helping your child to read

Kate Ruttle and Annemarie Young

OXFORD
UNIVERSITY PRESS

Contents

Level 4: Building Confidence in Reading is for children who:

- *can recognise 30–50 common words by sight*
- *can read harder sentences, with less support*
- *can use letter sounds to help make words*
- *can recognise more words in sentences*

Level 5: Reading with Confidence is for children who:

- *can recognise 50+ words by sight and use a range of strategies to work out unknown words*
- *express opinions about the characters and story*
- *read silently and begin to read ahead*
- *begin to attempt longer books*

Learning to read

Our aim in this Handbook is to show you how you can help
your child from an early age so that learning to read is
successful and enjoyable for you both. Children whose parents
help them at home have a huge advantage at school. This is
particularly true with reading, when time spent with your child
can help turn them into confident and successful readers.

From babyhood onwards, you can help your child to enjoy
books, to understand how books work, and to learn what it
means to be a 'reader'. There are many ways in which
you can help by playing games and doing activities,
as well as reading books together. This handbook
lists some ideas at each of the stages in a
child's early reading development.

As children learn to read, they need to
develop skills at many different levels.
Some people like to think of reading
as being about understanding the
'big shapes' (the meaning of sentences
and the shape of the story) and the
'little shapes' (individual words and
the letters used to make them).

In the early stages of learning to read, many children will show an initial preference for either the 'big shapes' or the 'little shapes', but we need to help children develop skills at the different levels. We can do this by reading with them and by:

- talking about stories and using story language
- using clues in the pictures to help them to understand the story
- using the 'context' (what comes before and after a word in the sentence or paragraph) to help make sense of the story

Kipper was fishing.

He got a hat.

- developing a knowledge of 'phonics' (how sounds are represented by individual letters and combinations of letters)
- helping them to recognise common words by sight so that they aren't having to struggle to work out all of the words in a sentence.

Some schools place more emphasis on one or other of these skills (for example, phonics or word recognition), but to become successful readers children need to learn to use all of them.

What does Read at Home provide?

Read at Home is closely linked to *Oxford Reading Tree*, the most successful reading scheme in the UK, which is used in over 80 per cent of primary schools and in many countries worldwide.

Read at Home features all the familiar *Oxford Reading Tree* characters in exciting new adventures which are written especially for you to enjoy with your children at home. Features include:

❧ carefully graded developmental levels (from 'Getting Ready to Read' for children aged 3+, to 'Reading with Confidence' for children aged 6+). Each level also has internal progression, from Book A to Book C.

Read at Home	Oxford Reading Tree
Level 1 Getting Ready	Stages 1 – 1+
Level 2 Starting to Read	Stages 2 – 3
Level 3 Becoming a Reader	Stages 3 – 4
Level 4 Building Confidence	Stages 4 – 5
Level 5 Reading with Confidence	Stages 5 – 7

❧ lots of opportunities for talking and sharing experiences. Each book also has puzzles and games.

❧ a strong focus on story, characters and humour (the 'big shapes') and a lot of repetition (the 'little shapes').

A Maze

Help the spaceship find its way through the fireballs to the Earth.

Getting children ready for reading

Listening to stories

From the time they are babies, you can help children to become readers by:

Dad got a duck!

- ◎ sharing your enjoyment of books
- ◎ reading stories and talking about the pictures
- ◎ comparing events in books with your own shared experiences
- ◎ pointing out signs and logos when you go shopping
- ◎ teaching them nursery rhymes and songs.

These simple activities help to prepare children for reading.

Starting to Read

When your child starts paying attention to the printed words in the book you are reading to them, they may be ready to start learning to read.

- ◎ Try to make time to read with your child every day.
- ◎ Read favourite stories again and again. Children love this.
- ◎ Build confidence by reading lots of books at the same reading level, and continue to re-read earlier books. If you push children to read books that are too hard, they are likely to lose interest.

Most important of all, if you are relaxed and enjoy reading with your child, that will pass on very strong messages about what fun reading is.

1

Level 1: Getting Ready to Read

How to support your child at this stage

Reading and enjoyment

Before they begin to join in with reading, children need to listen to stories, songs and rhymes, to join in with the telling of familiar stories, to handle books and enjoy looking at pictures. Be guided by their interests.

What skills do children need?

When they are at the 'Getting Ready to Read' stage of *Read at Home*, children can:

- ◎ enjoy sharing and talking about books
- ◎ recognise their own name
- ◎ match some words (for example, match *Mum* from a set of cards to the word *Mum* in a sentence)
- ◎ recognise some letter sounds (for example, some of the sounds in their name).

Mum

Mum was fishing.   She got a bucket.

Some of the activities on pages 14–15 will help to develop many of the skills children need in order to begin reading. At this early level, children's reading relies on the following:

- **Motivation** – if your child is inquisitive about how reading works, they will find the process much more interesting.
- **Memory** – don't be concerned if your child seems to be memorising rather than reading the book (and **please** don't cover up the pictures). Memory is a key skill for reading.
- **Concentration** – most children won't be ready to read until they can sustain concentration for 5–10 minutes.
- **Seeing and hearing** – in order to recognise the 'little shapes' in reading, children need to be good at identifying things that are the same or different.

Practical tips

Read with your child as often as you can: on the bus, in the bath, and in bed at night when you can make it special. Use the bedtime story as an opportunity to read *to* your child – they are usually too tired to read *with* you at that time.

Understanding print – story and meaning

Before you read a story with your child:

- talk about the title and the pictures on the cover
- look through the pictures together
- discuss what you think the story might be about.

11

Read the story to your child. (It's not cheating!)

- ◈ Don't stop to talk on the first read through.
- ◈ Point to the words as you read, matching one spoken word to one written word.

Re-read the story with your child, encouraging them to join in with repeated phrases.

◈ Talk about the pictures and discuss what's going to happen next.

He got a boot.

When you have finished reading, ask questions like:

◈ What was your favourite bit?

◈ Why do you think Floppy fell into the water?

◈ Has this ever happened to you?

There are suggested 'Think about the story' questions at the end of all the *Read at Home* books to help develop discussion and understanding.

Understanding print – words and letters

When you have read the story, you can then start to draw attention to the smaller shapes (words and letters).

- ⊗ Check that your child knows where to start reading and that the print is read from left to right.
- ⊗ Draw attention to the starting sound of a word and then ask them to find another word beginning with the same letter sound.
- ⊗ Ask them to find two words that are the same.

In all of the *Read at Home* books, there is a list of common useful words used in the book. (For a full list see page 30.) This shouldn't be used as a vocabulary test, but to help you when you are looking for other books your child might enjoy reading. The more practice they have at reading these words which appear frequently in children's reading and writing, the more likely they are to recognise them.

More ideas for reading at this level

Read as many books as you can, including:

- ⊗ retellings of traditional tales and fairy stories
- ⊗ familiar nursery rhymes
- ⊗ alphabet books
- ⊗ catalogues (Children love recognising things in them!)
- ⊗ classic books, like *Each Peach Pear Plum* by Alan and Janet Ahlberg and the *Cat on the Mat* books by Brian Wildsmith. Your local library will be able to help you.

Games and activities

Developing general skills for learning

There are many things you can do to help.

- Improve memory and concentration by playing simple card and board games, for example, Snap and Lotto. The *Read at Home Flashcards Word Games* provide ideas.

- Improve memory by playing Kim's Game: put four or five objects on a tray. Give your child time to look at them. Cover the tray and ask your child to name the objects.

- Develop sequencing and pattern-making skills, for example bead-threading to copy a pattern.

- Use drawing and tracing activities to focus on detail.

- Develop listening skills by using stories and nursery rhymes on tape and video.

Book-based activities

- Draw attention to special book language, like *Once upon a time* – it's not the same as spoken language.

- Talk about the books you are reading.

- Find books with characters they know. Many children will recognise Floppy, Kipper, Biff and Chip.

- Encourage children to retell favourite stories.

- Take your child to the library and encourage them to make choices about the books they want to read.

Picture activities

◎ Develop observation skills with, for example,

Find the feather hidden in every picture.

the 'Find the ... hidden' activities in the *Read at Home* books.

◎ Talk about the extra details in the pictures. *Oxford Reading Tree* and *Read at Home* stories usually include hidden bones and glasses and lots of visual jokes.

"Get that hat," said Kipper.

Biff ran.

Word activities

◎ Reading for meaning: look for words, signs and logos when you are out and about.

◎ Word building: use magnetic letters on the fridge and sponge letters in the bath.

◎ Use the *Read at Home Flashcards Word Games*.

Phonics activities

Encourage your child to recognise letters and rhymes.

◎ Recite rhymes they know, like *1, 2, 3, 4, 5, once I caught a fish…*, and get them to supply the rhyming word.

Level 2: Starting to Read

How to support your child at this stage

Reading and enjoyment

When you read aloud, include some books which are only slightly too hard for your child so that they can soon begin to read them.

Introduce paired reading, where you and your child read aloud together from the same familiar book. You can read more quietly as they become more confident.

What skills do children need?

When they are at the 'Starting to Read' stage of *Read at Home*, children are continuing to develop and refine all the skills from Level 1 (see pages 10–13). They should also be learning to:

- ◎ recognise a few common words by sight (for example, *said*)
- ◎ retell a simple story
- ◎ read a simple sentence using pictures to help
- ◎ recognise some letter sounds at the beginning of words (for example the 'd' in *dog*).

Practical tips

Always read a book aloud before you ask your child to read the book to you. This gives them the chance to understand the story, and to hear the words and language patterns.

Understanding print – story and meaning

◎ Talk about the title and cover pictures to predict what the story might be about.

◎ Point to the words as you read, matching one spoken word to one written word.

◎ Talk about what's happening and what will happen next.

When you have finished reading, ask questions like:

◎ *What was your favourite bit?*

◎ *Why did the tiger let Floppy go?*

There are suggested 'Think about the story' questions at the end of all the *Read at Home* books to help develop discussion and understanding.

"Look out!" said Floppy.
"There's a bee on your nose."

"Oh no!" said the tiger,
and he let Floppy go.

Understanding print – words and letters

Play word- and letter-spotting games like these with your child:

◎ *Can you find Floppy's name on this page?*

◎ *Can you find something in the picture that begins with the sound 'b'?*

More ideas for reading at this level

Read as many books as you can, including:

◎ retellings of traditional tales and fairy stories (for example, Aesop's *The Dog and the Bone*)

◎ familiar nursery rhymes (for example, *Nonsense Nursery Rhymes* by Richard Edwards)

◎ classic books, like *The Hungry Caterpillar* by Eric Carle.

Games and activities

Developing general skills for learning

Continue to play the games and activities suggested for Level 1 (pages 14–15), and introduce these new skills.

- Ⓢ Teach your child to recognise their own name, family names and family words like *Mum* and *Dad*.
- Ⓢ Use the *Read at Home Flashcards Word Games* to make sentences or to copy sentences from books.

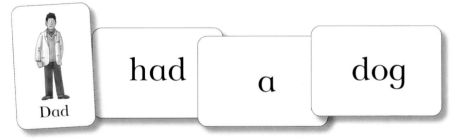

Story activities

- Ⓢ Ask children to draw pictures of their favourite storybook or TV characters and to talk about them.
- Ⓢ Invent new adventures for the characters together.

Picture activities

- Ⓢ Use sequences of pictures to tell stories.
- Ⓢ Talk about what a picture is 'about' to help your child to recognise the important elements.
- Ⓢ Play 'How many can you see?' games.

- Use the *Read at Home Flashcards Word Games* to play:
    - Snap (matching a limited number of words)
    - Memory game: turning over pairs of cards to find two that match.
- Look for words, signs and logos in the environment around you (restaurant names, shops, high street brands, 'P' for 'Parking', TV programmes and characters).

Phonics activities

- Play games like:
    - Sound sets: finding sets of words which begin or end with the same sound
    - Letter trains: making chains of words, matching the last letter of one with the first letter of the next.
- Play games like 'I spy with my little eye something beginning with 'a''.
- Sing the alphabet song.
- Play alliterative games, like 'Annie got an apple, Ben got a bike', etc.
- Use magnetic letters to make words. Copy words from the flashcards, rather than sounding out whole words.
- Use modelling clay or playdough to make letter shapes.
- Find pictures in magazines to make sets of 'Words which begin with…' and make an alphabet scrapbook.

(4–6-year olds)

Level 3: Becoming a Reader

How to support your child at this stage

Reading and enjoyment

When you read aloud, encourage your child to look at the words and pictures with you.

With paired reading (see page 16), let your child set the speed. When they hesitate, begin to say the first sound of the tricky word to help them.

What skills do children need?

When they are at the 'Becoming a Reader' stage of *Read at Home*, children still need to practise all the skills from the earlier levels (pages 10–13, 16–17). They should also be starting to:

- ◎ recognise 10–20 common words by sight
- ◎ read simple sentences
- ◎ recognise all the letter sounds at the beginning of words
- ◎ use some expression when they re-read books.

Practical tips

- ◎ Look at the pictures together before you read, discussing what you think the story might be about.

"Look at that," said Dad.
"Dogs can't go on the sand."

"Poor Floppy!" said Mum.
"I'll take him for a walk."

20

- Read aloud any words that might be tricky.
- Read any repeated phrases. This will help your child recognise them when they read the book on their own.

Understanding print – story and meaning

Continue with all the earlier activities.

- Talk about all the events in the story: *What happened first? Then what happened? What happened in the end?*
- Help them to talk about their feelings about the story.

If your child loses the meaning of what they are reading, ask them to stop and think about what the word or sentence might mean, using a variety of strategies:

- reading to the end of the sentence and then deciding on a sensible word to fill the gap
- re-reading the sentence
- using the picture
- using the letter sounds.

If they still can't read the word, read it for them.

Understanding print – words and letters

- Point out letters that go together, for example, *th*, *sh*.
- Draw your child's attention to speech marks, punctuation, sound effects and action words (for example, *BUMP*, *ZOOM*).

ZOOM! Floppy flew the spaceship out of danger. "Phew! Just in time," he said.

Read as many books as you can at a similar reading level.

Games and activities

Continue to play the games and activities suggested for Levels 1 and 2 (pages 14–15, 18–19), and introduce these new skills.

Story activities

◎ Talk about what might happen after the story ending.

> Where do spaceships go in space? Where would you like to go?

◎ Together, write captions for photographs of your child playing with a friend, doing craft activities, etc. to provide a motivating and personal book.

◎ Introduce simple non-fiction books, so your child can see that books have many different purposes.

◎ Introduce simple rhyme books (for example, *Dr Seuss*).

Picture activities

◎ Make up your own story to go with wordless books like *The Snowman* by Raymond Briggs.

Use *Read at Home Flashcards Word Games* to play games:

- ◎ Choose two or more words from a selection. Can your child say a sentence containing those words?

- ◎ Write a sentence, but miss out one word. Can they choose a word that could fill the gap from a set of words?

- ◎ Give them a page from a magazine. How many common words like *but, come, want,* etc. can they recognise?

- ◎ Put a selection of words out and say a sentence using one or more of the words. Can your child hand you the flashcards for those words?

Phonics activities

- ◎ When you play *I spy*, include words that begin with two consonants, for example, *br, cl, dr, st*; words that end with two consonants, for example, *nd, st, lk*; or words that rhyme.

- ◎ Use magnetic letters. Build a word and ask your child to make a word that rhymes, or is one letter different, or begins or ends with the same letter.

- ◎ Show your child one of the flashcard words. How many times can they write it in one minute?

said

Level 4: Building Confidence in Reading and
Level 5: Reading with Confidence

How to support your child at these stages

Reading and enjoyment

Try sharing a book together – you read one page and your child reads the next. This has three main advantages:

◎ You are modelling what fluent reading sounds like.

◎ The book is completed more quickly, and your child is more likely to want to re-read it. (You can swap pages.)

◎ If your child loses the meaning of the story while they concentrate on reading their pages, they can pick up the meaning again while you are reading.

What skills do children need?

When children are Building Confidence in Reading, Level 4 of *Read at Home*, they still need to practise all the skills from the earlier levels. They should also be learning to:

◎ recognise 30–50 common words by sight

◎ read harder sentences, with less support

◎ use letter sounds to help make words

◎ recognise more words in sentences.

When children are Reading with Confidence, Level 5 of *Read at Home*, they should be able to:

- recognise 50+ words and use a range of strategies to work out unknown words
- express opinions about the characters and story
- read silently and begin to read ahead
- begin to attempt longer books.

Practical tips

Understanding print – story and meaning

Children who are reading at these stages should be encouraged to:

- re-read the text when it doesn't make sense
- work out tricky words, using meaning and pictures as well as phonics
- make links between events in books and their own lives (*I remember when…*)
- use expression when re-reading a text.

Understanding print – letters and words

- Help children to focus on chunks in words, rather than individual letter sounds, for example *bark/ed.*
- When your child is stuck on a word, help them to:

  - sound out chunks of the word
  - re-read the sentence to create a meaningful context
  - read on to the end of the sentence.

Read as many books as you can at this level.

Games and activities

Continue to play the games and activities suggested for the earlier levels (pages 14–15, 18–19, 22–23), and introduce these new skills.

Story activities

◈ Encourage your child to write their own short stories with your help.

◈ Ask them to think beyond the text and think about how characters might feel and what they might think at different times in the story.

◈ Ask your child to retell stories from TV programmes and videos you have watched.

◈ Encourage your children and their friends to do puppet shows, plays, etc. for you to watch.

Picture activities

◈ Encourage your child to 'read' the pictures in books they can't yet read. How much can they find out? Can they produce their own version of the story?

◈ Introduce your child to famous paintings by making up stories together based on the pictures.

Word activities

- Use *Read at Home Flashcards Word Games* activities.

- Make jumbled words. For example, cut out the letters from a word like *some* and ask your child to rebuild the word.

- Build vocabulary: *I went shopping and I got an amazing anteater; a beautiful bike; colourful crayons,* etc. (alliterative adjectives).

Phonics activities

- Your child should now be familiar with words that read as they sound, for example, *cat,* so start pointing out tricky words which you can't sound out.
    - Which words look as if they should rhyme, but don't? For example, *home, come; do, no.*
    - Which words rhyme, even though they look different? For example, *come, sum; there, bear, hair.*

The more children read, the more confident and successful they will become as readers. Keep reading and enjoying books together even when your child is reading fluently.

Questions parents often ask

It's never too early. Babies and toddlers enjoy looking at picture books and hearing them read aloud. Chant nursery rhymes, sing songs and share picture books from birth onwards!

Yes. Teach the alphabet through songs and games, but focus more on letter sounds rather than names when you're doing reading activities. Encourage children to learn both letter names and letter sounds, with magnetic letters, and games like *I spy*.

In many early reading books, the pictures are much more interesting than the text! Continue to read stories to your child as they focus on the pictures. Most of the story-based activities in this Handbook concentrate on overall meaning and understanding, and can be taught through pictures. Focus on the words and letters through the word and phonics activities.

Don't discourage them. It's good to have favourite books, and reading familiar stories gives them confidence.

When and how can I ask my child to start trying to read with me?

Be guided by your child – don't force the pace too early or you risk putting them off. Re-read the advice on pages 10–13. If your child isn't ready, spend more time reading to them and playing games. If they're asking what words say, they're probably ready to begin. Start with a familiar story (for example, *Goldilocks*) with lots of repeated phrases. The *Read at Home* stories have lots of repetition and patterning.

What if my child makes a mistake while they're reading?

Don't stop the flow of the reading unless what they've read doesn't make sense. The meaning is the most important thing in reading in the early stages, and accuracy will come.

What should I do if they get stuck on a word?

In the early stages, quietly say the word. Later:

- encourage them to refer to the picture
- get them to try the first sound of the word
- break the word into chunks (syllables)
- get them to read the whole sentence and then ask them to guess the word. Focus on the meaning.

What if my child seems to stop making progress?

Don't worry. Children develop at different speeds and they always need to consolidate what they are learning before moving on. Continue to re-read familiar books, introduce new books at the same level, play the games and always be encouraging. Once they are ready, progress will resume.

Don't put pressure on them or you will spoil the fun!

Home–School Links

When your child starts school, continue to read to and with them as often as you can.

- Make use of home/school reading records to share your child's achievements and worries about reading.
- Talk to the teacher if you feel that a book is too hard or too easy for your child. There's usually a good reason why they've been given a particular book.
- Continue to read a wide range of books as well as your child's reading books. Use activities from this Handbook to extend your child's enjoyment of their reading book.

100 Common Useful Words used in the *Read at Home* stories

a, after, all, am, an, and, another, at, away, back, ball, been, began, big, but, can, can't, children, cold, come, could, Dad, didn't, do, dog, family, fast, find, for, get, go, going, good, got, had, has, he, help, here, him, his, I, in, is, it, just, know, like, look, looking, let's, make, me, Mum, must, my, need, no, not, of, on, out, over, play, pull, push, ran, said, saw, see, she, so, some, someone, something, stop, suddenly, surprise, take, that, the, them, they, there, this, thought, to, took, up, very, wants, was, we, went, were, what, where, with, yes, you

Useful Contacts offering advice on reading

Booktrust produces booklists and other information. www.booktrusted.co.uk Tel: 020 8516 2977

British Dyslexia Association is the national organisation for specific learning difficulties. www.bda-dyslexia.org.uk Tel: 0118 966 8271 (helpline)

Oxford University Press Find out more about the *Oxford Reading Tree* at www.OxfordPrimary.com

The Parent Centre is the Department for Education and Skills website for all parents and carers. www.parentcentre.gov.uk

Reading is Fundamental is an initiative of the National Literacy Trust (www.literacytrust.org.uk). RiF promotes reading for pleasure and offers parents advice and support. www.rif.org.uk Tel: 020 7828 2435